A
Heart
Unveiled

To Know Him

Angela Q. Bertone

For information and inquiries contact Angela Q. Bertone P. O. Box 2124,

Ponchatoula, LA 70454

www.angelabertone.com

Authored by Angela Q. Bertone

Paperback ISBN

ISBN-13: **978-0692580967 (Ask Angela Productions LLC)**

ISBN-10: **0692580964**

Kindle ASIN: B0181MCG5A

If we suffer with Him,
we shall reign with Him.

Thank you Father for teaching me
the mysteries of suffering with you
to know you.

ANGELA Q. BERTONE

A Heart Unveiled

To Know Him

By Angela Q. Bertone

TABLE OF CONTENTS

Hear, Here Comes the Bride   9

Passions Beyond the Grave   13

"Mercy" I Cry   15

Princess Merab

and The Whisper on

the Wind *The Bride's Song*   17

Your Heart In Me   21

Awake   22

That I Might Know You   23

Christ In Me   25

He Looks Like You   27

Will You Know Me?   29

Hear My Cry   31

The Affection Due Her   32

Understanding   33

Glory Sings   34

The Bride's Cry *Passion or Death*   35

Slumber Love   36

You Alone	37
It Ain't What You Think It Is	38
My One Desire	39
A Spotless Bride	40
Move Us I Pray	42
I Am Just A Man	43
Fire Deep Within My Bones	44
A Cup Pure And Old	45
Towers Twin Fall	47
The Hero's Wives	48
Rain On Me	49
Gotta Run	50
No One Can Compare	51
Ever Blowing Wind	52
Remember Me In My Travail	53
Shadows	54
Thine Eyes	55
Walk Upon The Water	58
Two Sides	59
Blameless	60
The Peace Where Love Is Found	61

Oil Power Forth   62

In The Heart of Man   63

He Is My Strength   64

Cover Me   65

His Will Fulfilled   67

Loss Child's Cry   70

Her Blood Cried "Mercy"   78

Postscript   82

About the Author   83

Hear, Here Comes the Bride

For the longest time, I have desired to be your soul's provider. Say you will let Me, and I will. It has been Our Father's will since before time. I know time has seemed to stand still, but He and I are time, and We invite you to enter into eternity and let Us be your soul's provider. We have longed to protect you from the thorns of the cursed tree, but you would not. Has time changed your mind? Are you ready for love? Has the darkness ravished you long enough? Has the winter frozen you in time? Know ye not, that the winter only causes the bud to spring forth at the rising of the sun? Spring needs your desire to live. Can you hear My call? Are you in need of my touch to awaken? Does not My voice beckon your wings to fly? They were sealed in amber passions that if aroused, are able to melt the darkness of winter.

Say you remember Love. For Love never ends. Grab hold of it quickly and don't let go. Remember love, and desire shall spark the amber that has sealed the wings of your heart. Breathe the breath of passion, and burn once again. I shall wait forever for your love, and after our embrace, it shall seem as a vapor the waiting.

In My waiting, time appears frozen. If you are not able to hear My voice, then feel the vibration as My love shakes the earth. Love is the fire that can melt any darkness. So, I take the risk. I gamble on love. This day, this moment, I shall speak and shake all that can be shaken. I have left My soul in you as an earnest deposit, and I must forfeit My essence if My promises are not true. Oh, but you know that there is no darkness in Me, and My words are true. Love never fails. Though a mother forsakes her child or the mountains fall into the sea, My love shall abide for always. You are to Me forever and always.

You were sent to Me in a dream, and in a word, from My Father's lips, and He is forever faithful and true. Your face is like the sun, able to chase the winter away with the passion of your soul. Even death cannot erase our love. For this love is without measure.

If My words you cannot hear, then I shall write it to you in the sky. The oceans shall carry the Truth and deposit it on every shore. Upon the wind I have left My fragrance and in every song I will hide My voice. The ready writer's pen shall declare the Way. The depth of your love shall be revealed, for My Father has declared it to be so.

The winter may have slowed your memories, but Love never fails. So yet again, I refuse to let the sun go down on My wrath. My anger from the breath of My nostrils shall cause fear and the terror of the night winds to crumble like the dust. Darkness has been upon your face for far too long, so again I say: "Let there be light" and the mountains did melt like wax.

The storm began to rage. Sea bellows roared and the ice glaciers released their foundation and floated away. The fire from our souls caused the ice to melt, and smoke filled the air, covering the landscape.

"Arise!" I cried, and I saw her hand.

I reached across time and did grasp it.   Cold as ice, I held it tight. No longer shall I wait, and never shall I let go. The fire from My heart sent a bolt of life and jolted her free. Her form sprang from the frozen ground and I heard her breath.

Color washed over her gray form and the earth cried, "She is alive!"

"Groan no longer inhabitants of the earth, for spring is here."

Suddenly the eyes of the earth were flooded with the light of our love. The flowers came from their hiding place and sang hallelujah. The turtle dove flew with the branch of the olive tree and dripped the oil thereof on her brow.

The evergreen quickly covered her nakedness and the handmaidens rushed to her side. They summoned the eagles who fed her fresh meat. The grapevines surrendered and she did drink. The clouds formed her wedding gown and robed her in humility. The veil of grace that covered her face was lifted by her Father.

"Who gives this woman?" the forest asked.

"Her mother and I," replied the Ancient of Days.

"Who takes this woman?" the wind whispered.

"I do," said the Son.

The Bride stepped forth and took His hand. Manifestations filled the land. The sons of God now made known. Heaven on earth, and in the midst of them, a throne. The galaxies gathered to witness and testify for none could hold their peace. "WHOLY, WHOLY!" the whole earth cried. The Father's Will revealed!

Passions Beyond the Grave

I feel the trembling like a whirlwind in my soul. My hands begin to sweat, and I feel my heart in my throat. *Breathe!* I tell myself, *breathe*. Memories of my past flood my mind and tell me lies. Lies and more lies. Whom shall I believe and of whom shall I be afraid? Who dares to be my enemy when my God is for me? Is there any who can stand in His presence? Let Him speak now, or forever hold His peace.

Is there nothing that He will not use to bless me, and reveal His never-ending love for me? Who dares to defile the Bride of the Living God? The Ancient of Days has called and has chosen her. He has called her by her name, and He alone has ordained her destiny. For her days were numbered before time existed. Her groom was slain before the foundations were laid, and she too was crucified with Him, and in Him, and forever shall she remain in Him.

He foreknew her, and did predestine her to reign with Him at His side. Because of His love, no fear can abide in her, for she only has eyes for Him. When she does tremble, it is at His presence. For His essence is her breath, and the life of her. He alone can satisfy her soul.

Oh, it is true she did run in times past, and tasted of what could never fill her soul, but only to remind her of who she is, and who she was created to be. For He has no fear. Her

Freedom cannot rob Him of her eternal desires for Him. Though temporary temptations did confuse her, and cause her eyes to be blind, though the illusions crippled her legs, and hardened her heart for a season, know ye not that it is His hands that formed her and it is His hands that formed her yet again.

He has removed her heart of stone, and did give her a heart of flesh. He has filled it with His spirit, and set her ablaze. Passions beyond the grave did awaken her soul, and never again shall she roam. She has found her home in Him, and her eyes are now fixed; fixed on His love, and have been made into diamonds. His light is in her eyes, and they do shine forth His glory.

Like the moon, she has no light of her own, yet she willingly reflects the light of the Son. He has clothed her in humility by way of the law and judgment. She delights in Him alone.

She bears in her soul the sons of men lost in sin, and she cries for their return home. Her Father she longs for, and to please His soul is her destiny.

Many are the sons and daughters of the promise, and nothing is impossible for Him. For He alone is God, and His eyes are never dim. He is the beginning and the end, and time does not bind the Almighty. He holds it in His hands as a deposit of change.

Ring the bells, and sound the trumpets! Let all the Heavens and the Earth rejoice! The time has come and the time is now. Sing, oh sing aloud! Here comes the Bride. Make it known in the heavens, and now in the earth. Reveal, Reveal, Reveal! Let the mysteries be seen. Let every tongue rejoice and declare Him, King of Kings.

"Mercy!" I Cry

What is reason, and why have I clung to it for so long? Reason has left me in the dust and on my belly, I did crawl. I beat my head upon the rock, and reason did die. Now I am blind and deaf, for my head I have lost.

Do not weep for me. It is not Your pity that I desire. Rather love me, and give me Your eyes. Marry me, and be my head. Cover me, for I lay naked. My form has been twisted by the night reasons, and I long to be made straight. Feed my soul, for I have no mouth and my words have died. Take me, and consume me, that I may live inside of You and no longer to self-abide.

In my reason, I became one with death, but my worm refused to die. So, by my own hand, I surrendered and cut off my head. For I would rather die, than stay bound to my reasons.

Now that my head is cut off, I cry with my heart, "Be the breath of me. Be my head. Marry me, that I may live again. Have mercy on me, and cover me in grace. Be my eyes, be my ears, be the words in my mouth."

I did not fashion the oceans, yet I long to hold the hand that holds the ocean in them. I have neither thunder nor lightning, yet I long for Your words to be in my mouth. There are no stars in my eyes for I have cut off my head, and my eyes are no longer among the living.

You, You have fire in Your eyes. Be my eyes I pray. Take my form, and crush me now. Take my twisted form that has been covered in this darkness, and light my way. "All things are possible for You," I have heard the heavens say.

Would You make me dust and make me new? Is it possible to find beauty in my ashes? Oh, that You would put me on the altar, and burn away my chaff. Take my form and consume it. Pour in fresh oil and form me anew. Take away my scales, no longer to measure. Rather, give me wings and put Your secret in my soul. The secret of the heavens, the secrets of love.

Does not even the earth give forth fruit when Your words are spoken, "Be fruitful and multiply"? Would You not crush me, and make me new? Bury this form. Does not Your Word say, "From dust you came, and to dust you shall return"?

Remove my grave clothes and give me wings. For this worm in me refuses to die. Do not even the insects that are here today, and gone tomorrow take wings and fly? Were they not once a worm, like unto me?

"Mercy, mercy and grace!" I cry. Crush me and make me new. Find wings for me and let me fly.

Consume me in Your fire, and let me abide upon the altar. Melt me like butter, and dip Your bread in me. Take me, break me, and give me away. Mold me and use me, for Your kingdom I pray. For I have found You, and I know You are true. You are faithful and loving, and I give myself to You.

Princess Merab and
the Whisper on the Wind

The Bride's Song

"Feel freedom whenever you want. You can call on Me anytime."

The harvest and new beginning are here by the way of grace; the grace of our God, for the fullness of God and man has come.

"The completion of time has beckoned the trumpets to sound, causing my heart to beat like a war drum, echoing in my chest. I can't wait to see You face to face, and to see all that Father has ordained. Over the cliff I go. I see love in Your eyes. You nailed it again. The words perfect and the vibrations in the song are heavenly."

"What are you doing? Are you ready to drink from this cup? Yes, it is bitter, but you like coffee with sugar and cream. Are you able to transcend? Remember, I am time and space, and you can trust Me."

"Come, go away with Me!" I heard Him say.

"Who do you speak of?" I heard my sisters say.

"My Beloved," was my reply.

"What did you drink?" they asked, "For your lover we have not seen. Are you drunk?"

"Yes!" I replied, "Drunk with His essence."

"I know you are sleeping but I have found Him and of this Love I must tell. Last night while I slept, I dreamed a dream. My lover came to me from within my heart, and I heard the sound of Love. It became my very breath, and now He is all I can see."

"I saw myself in His eyes, and I am smitten. You were with me. I saw you there. Don't you remember? He made a river with His hands, and we all did swim. He made us clean, and gave us new clothes to wear. It was our birthday, and He rejoiced over us, and it pleased Him to give us our desires. His fragrance is as the cedars, and it is called pleasure. While we were swimming, He stepped away, and I left you in the water to go look for Him."

"He left His fragrance blowing in the wind, and I could not resist, so I followed. I think He made wings and flew away, but I heard Him whisper on the wind, *'Come follow me'*."

"But then I heard the water fall, and the rain, and I lost His whisper on the wind. Please tell me you have seen Him."

"We see nothing sister. you must be sick. Take rest, and we shall prepare food for you."

"No!" I replied, "He shall feed me. I shall search all night if I must. I shall find Him, or die in pursuit of Him. For you have spoken the truth, I am sick. I am homesick, and He has come for me."

Through the valleys, and over the hills I searched and my clothes have become tattered. The night grabbed at me, and tormented my mind, spilling darkness upon my skin. I came to a river laden with lilies, and I did collapse as a corpse. An angel came and covered me, and gave me a smooth stone for my head. I looked, and I saw two eagles had covered me to protect me from the night beast.

In my tears, I cried, "He loves me. He shall find me, for my heart tells me so."

"These lilies shall be for my grave or my wedding; for without Him I would choose death. He comes for me, for I know His love conquers all."

"He shall not leave my soul in hell, for He too is love sick, for I have seen His eyes. His love is sure; so now, I must rest. For I am weary, and heavy laden, and He shall give me rest."

I wait at the threshold of Canaan, where He shall part the waters, and carry me over. He shall take me into His chambers, and clean me with myrrh. In the *mourning* I shall awake and behold His glory. His glorious face. For I hear His footsteps in the beating of my heart.

I took a breath, and thought it was my last; until I heard Him call my name.

"Beloved ...It is I. I Am here. Awake sleepy eyes, and let Me look at you."

"Turn away," I cried. For the night has covered me, and caused my skin to darken. My garments are torn, and tattered, please look away."

He breathed on me. A river flowed from my soul and I was clean. He kissed my head, and healed my wounds. He touched my cheek bone, and my hair began to shine like the sun. He turned my eyes upward, and I looked into His marvelous face. I looked, and beheld His glory and I cried "Holy!"

Smoke flamed from His nostrils, and wedding garments replaced my threads. He lifted my head from the rock, and placed a lily in my hair. He carried me across the threshold, and onto the shores of Canaan. There He breathed the breath of life into my lungs, and kissed me with the kisses of His mouth. I became lifeless in His arms, and He kissed me again. The fire from His eyes pierced mine, and we became one.

I only have eyes for Him, and He spoke again and said unto me, 'The springtime is here, and the turtle doves are calling. Will you go away with me?'

"Yes!" I cried. "Yes!" And we flew away.

He is calling. He is calling! Ooh, oh, sound the call, for today the day has come; and today the time is now, to enter into the rest of Him.

"Come go away with me!"

Your Heart in Me

Oh God, how I took what was holy and I profaned it. But You saw me and had pity on me and in Your compassion, You made Your heart of grief known to me.

You restored me beneath the cloud of my cries and the river of my tears. Your fire consumes me, and in Your presence, I live though I was dead. For You loved me and knew me.

You are the Spirit of Truth and it is no longer I that live – but Christ who lives – now lives in me. It is now Your heart, Your joys, Your sorrows that dwell in me.

Therefore, oh soul of mine, let God arise and His enemies be scattered!

Awake

Arise, awake, shine! Oh, Word of God be restored unto me. Live, make war! Let it be known unto all the inhabitants of the earth what the glory of the Lord is.

Make me your warrior. Inhabit His vessel.

Shine, shine, shine, be seen among the nations. Wake the hearts of men. Call us from our slumber. Open our eyes that we can see the manifested glory of our God.

Make our hearts cry out. For we are longing for You. Break forth from the soil of our souls and bring forth a harvest.

That I Might Know You

I came down to you

that I might know you.

If you had to suffer, if you had to die,

So would I, that I might know you.

Because you would be rejected,

Because you would be lonely,

Because you would be abandoned,

So would I, that I might know you.

Because you would be mocked,

Because you would be separated and betrayed,

So would I that I might know you.

I came down to you, that I might know you.

If you have to suffer, if you had to die,

So would I, that I might know you.

Because you left your place of safety,

Because you left your place of love,

Because you left the place of the Father,

so would, I that I might know you.

Because you needed forgiveness,

Because you needed My life,

Because you need to know the Father to have eternal life.

I came down to you, that I might know you. If you have to suffer, if you had to die, So would I.

Christ in Me

It is Christ in you. Christ in me. He is our hope;

He is our glory.

Let God arise.

It's no longer us that live.

It's no longer me.

Our life is not our own.

His breath is in you. His breath is in me.

Our breath is not our own.

Let God arise.

It's no longer what you feel.

It's no longer me.

Our feelings are not our own.

His joy in us, His grief alone.

Our feelings are not our own.

Let God arise.

It is Christ in you. Christ in me.

He is our hope. He is our glory.

Let God arise.

Christ in you. Christ in me.

Our life is not our own.

He Looks Like You

When I look at you, I see Him. His glorious image covers you. My heart sings out, "Lord my Lord, He looks like you. He is my gift, my picture, He is my personal image of you."

When I touch you, I can feel Him. His strength covers your frame. I feel His power; I feel His tenderness. When I touch you I think of His Name.

Lord my Lord, He looks like you. He is my gift, my picture; He is my personal image of you. Lord my Lord He looks like you.

When I taste love on your lips, the sweetness of oneness. When I'm filled with your presence, I am mystified. My soul cries, "Lord my Lord, He looks like you. He is my gift, my picture; He is my personal image of you."

When you hold me, I smell your scent. Your fragrance awakens my Heart. I can breathe the same breath and our souls are one.

Abiding in our hearts, we travel in to eternity where time appears to vanish. Lord my Lord, He looks like you. He is my gift, my picture; He is my personal image of you.

When I hear your voice, soft and strong, deep from inside your soul; my heart stops, and my soul receives the sound, and the pounding of my heart begins. I wait for a word; a part of you, poured out for me. I receive your heart into mine, a voice of unity.

ANGELA Q. BERTONE

Lord my Lord, He looks like you. He is my gift; my picture; He's my personal image of you. Lord my Lord, He looks like you.

Will You Know Me?

Do you hear Me? Am I getting through to you? Can you hear Me? Do you know I'm inside of you? I am speaking. I am as close as I can be. I'm inside of you. Can you feel Me?

I am touching inside of you. I am writing, I am writing inside of you. I am giving, giving Myself to you. Will you hear Me? Will you listen to Me speak? Will you hear Me?

Are you willing to feel My pain? Will you know Me? I want to know you. I want to know you. Will you know Me? I have the morning and the night. I hold the stars shining bright. I smile and a sunset is seen. I am, and the moon beams.

Without you, I long. I am longing for you. I have the riches of existence, and I hold time in My hand. The waters obeyed Me, and still I made man. For without you I long. I'm longing for you. I am Life. I am Light. I am Breath, and I am. Yet without you I long. I am longing for you.

The oceans roar, and the wind is like it. The angels bow at My feet. Praise is ever before Me; yet without you I long. I am longing for you.

Would you hold My heart in your hand? Even though you are just a man. Would you touch Me, feel My pain? Can you hear Me calling your name?

Who can know Me? Who will understand? Who can find Me where I am?

There is no mountain, there is no morning who can know Me. Would you hold My heart in your hand, would you know Me?

I have made My home inside of you; yet you refuse to know Me. You push Me away, and then call My Name. Would you hold My heart and feel My pain? Reach deep inside, and call My name?

Knowing Me will hurt, for My pain is great, but not worthy to be compared to the glory. Will you know Me?

Hear My Cry

Oh Father, I am blind. I can't see. My ears reach out to silence. I breathe and smell the death of my soul. I tried to run to you, but I can feel nothing. I long, and reach to taste His sweetness, but I only find my deadness.

My heart breaks at my death. The cry pierces my soul. I am poured out as a drink offering, with only death to offer. My heart cries out for mercy. Though only a part of my body can move and feel.

"Hear me," I cry. "Hear me please. Though my cry be small and faint, only you can know me in my state."

"Heal me, I pray! I long to see, that I might see Your love. I long to hear, that you might say 'Be whole.' I long to breathe, only your breath. I long to feel, and touch your face. I long to taste, your sweet grace. Hear my cry! Mercy! Mercy!"

The Affection Due Her

The affection due her, the love of your life, to know and understand her, your soul mate, your wife.

A man of understanding fears the Lord. A man of understanding can conquer the world.

His hands are soft when they touch. His strength no words can describe how much. He knows the difference between love and lust. He understands her need for a simple soft touch.

When her heart is full of love, honor and respect, she longs for her husband to make her complete. The coming together, an expression of oneness, is something a woman cannot resist.

The affection due her, the love of your life, to know and understand her, your soul mate, your wife.

To look into her eyes until your souls meet; in a moment of time, she feels complete. To caress her face, and hold her hand, she needs to be held by a godly man. In his heart and arms, she finds the affection due her.

Let us open our hearts, share our joys and pain. Let us grow together, and unite as one. This love we share is rarely seen. It is our gift to cherish, a gift from our King.

A picture of His love, a great mystery: the affection due her, the love of your life, to know and understand her, your soul mate, your wife.

Understanding

A moment of understanding, a power inside. Emotions turning as the ocean's tide. A wondering, an awakening, an opening of the eyes.

Painful, hurting, grief inside. A moment of understanding, a power inside. Awaken in the ***mourning*** as the Son rises. A new day dawning, a new light shining.

Facing the Son, the light so bright. Facing the Son, leaving the night. Turning, turning as the earth is turning, so am I.

Misunderstanding, division, pain, ripping, tearing, sin, shame. Seeking for oneness, unity. Seeking a freedom for you and me.

Inward feeling. Touching the pain. Inward feeling. Seeing my shame. Fire, fire, burning deep. Changing, changing setting me free.

Wisdom, knowledge? Fear the Lord. See Him, touch Him as He carries your pain. Do not miss understanding!

Glory Sings

All around me glory sings. **Son** rays, light beams.

In darkness I groped for so long. In darkness I

walked singing songs.

My deafness rang in my ears, not knowing in silence, I was
one with fear.

Yet, You called me by my name, at the opening of my ears
and eyes, I saw my shame.

As I cried in deep despair, Your grace covered me, though
I was bare.

Your love poured forth as mercy flowed. Your greatness,
Your glory I now know.

All around me glory sings.

The Bride's Cry

Passion or Death

Give me passion or give me death. I long for passion more than my breath. The fire in me needs to burn. To know You, is my heart's only yearn. Knowing You, to hear You whisper in my ear, is worth more than a life filled with years.

Give me passion or give me death! Be my breath!

I must feel Your heart in mine: the longing inside is the love for new wine. Pour Yourself in me, is what I ask. Give me passion or give me death!

My longing lives in me to smell Your sweetness; to hear Your voice; to feel Your touch; to see   Your face; to taste of Your grace... without You my life is waste.

Give me passion or give me death!

Slumber Love

"In the stillness of night, Your warmth is around me. I rest in peace, just knowing You are there. As I slumber with You at my side, no fear can enter my heart."

"I turn in sleepy love and find You are there. You reach out and touch my face and stroke my hair. My hand in Yours, I slumber again, until my heart awakens me: a fire inside, burning, burning brighter still. When at last we meet in a holy place as we linger until."

"You take me places I've never seen. A love ever changing, every growing – deeper without end. In the stillness of night, I rest with You in peace forevermore."

You
Alone

When I look into Your eyes I see the Truth that sets me free. When I feel Your power and strength, I rest in perfect peace.

To hear Your voice, like thunder rolling – it takes away my breath, just the knowing. Softly, You touch my heart, yet I break at the mention of Your Name. You alone can take me to places where I can face my shame.

Before You alone I am bare. My nakedness covers me, yet You embrace me with tender care. You robe me undefiled with Your righteousness, for You alone can know me.

It Ain't What You Think It Is

It ain't what you think it is. It ain't what you see. It's different than I thought it was. It's as deep as the seas.

I thought it was this way and then found it to be that. When I thought I was going forward, I was only going back.

All the things I thought I knew, all that I had learned was found to be rubbish, a walk, a wish; then my eyes were opened. I saw things I had never seen.

It ain't what you think it is – Oh God, help us see.

My One Desire

Perfect in me all Your works and all Your words. Fulfill Yourself in me. Your heart oh God, let me not fail.

My love for You is limited I know, but You can change me and make me new. You can make me love like You.

Here I am, have Your way. Though through the fire I must go. I trust You God with all my heart. I give unto You my breath. Take all of me until there is nothing left, for You alone can change me into Your desire. Pour Yourself in me with Your all- consuming fire.

Be in me, my all in all. Fulfill Your Word with Your mighty power. You, You God, You alone are my one desire. Change me! Make me a flaming fire.

Have Your way with me, and so let it be on earth as it is in heaven.

A Spotless Bride

A spotless bride, who is she?   The one without wrinkle –
blameless she will be.

Where can she be found? Who is like unto thee? The eyes
of heaven search and the eyes of the earth; where oh
where?

Open all eyes. Let this mystery be seen: a wife, a fire,
hidden. Open the seals. Let revelation be!

Then, the winds blew away all the chaff. Lightening like
revelation fell from heaven, and sparked the forest of men.
A blaze was seen in the midst of them: One whose passion
burned so fierce no judgment could stand. Understanding
like a blanket of smoke filled the heavens, and covered the
land.

The accuser ran from the flames, but had nowhere to run.
The flames were so great; they went wherever the wind did
blow. All accusations were then consumed, and the
knowledge of good and evil was seen.   All the eyes of
men were opened, and all the mysteries were revealed.

The rains of heaven began to fall; the latter rains proclaimed. The waters of heaven fell like a flood, and covered all the earth again.

Unlike the flood of Noah's days, mankind was not destroyed. But in this flood the covenant was seen, and fulfilled. All sin and evil were destroyed and only Love remained.

Where could such a storm come from? What made this great rain fall?

It fell from the heart of God, when the bride came to call.

Move Us, I Pray

This is a prayer that I wrote one Sunday morning after a word of the Lord came forth, but none was moved.

Oh Lord my God, my heart is filled with such sorrow. Forgive us, for when You speak, our ears are deaf. We speak with our lips and say we want You. We pray and ask You to speak. Yet, when You speak, we are not moved by Your words. Life goes on as usual. We strive to keep order, "our order", thinking it is to honor You. However, we have failed to understand that to honor You is to know You. Open our ears, that we might hear You and that Your words would move us to change. Oh God, be God in our hearts and deliver us from the traditions of men.

I Am Just a
Man

Oh, that I could see Your face. If only I could see. I cried out with a loud voice, "Son of David, have mercy on me!"

He bid me come and opened my eyes. The light so bright, shown from His face, my wretchedness was all I could see: what shame, what guilt, unspeakable grief. I hung my head in disbelief.

The Son of God before me stood, with mercy in His eyes. Oh, the love and grace like a river flowed. In my ultimate wretched state, His love is all that showed.

Before this day I dreamed of sight; the day mine eye could see. Yet in my deepest, and wildest dreams I never knew that it could be, so great and awesome, mighty and strong to see the Son of Man. To know and see myself just as I am; poor and wretched in the face of God.

This was His plan to feel the river of His love…. for I am just a man.

Fire Deep Within My Bones

Desire in me burns like fire, deep within my bones. Fire from above; a love I had never known.

This kind of love reminds me of a dream while still a little girl. The dream of a fairytale princess where love is ever in bloom. Where flowers sweet fill the air as gentle breezes blow, and sunlight dances on the dew and offers a glistening glow.

Desire in me rises high; higher and higher still. Where something from within me causes me to yield.

All my being is on a quest, though life itself is lost. For this desire must be filled, nothing too great a cost. This desire in me is only to know Him unyielding, unstoppable, until all is fulfilled.

This desire is so heavenly; I dare not call it my own. For only God could place a fire so deep within my bones.

So, this quest continues until I see His face. My only quest is to know Him and taste His precious grace.

A Cup Pure and Old

Betrayal came before mine eyes to place its hooks in me.

"Oh, no!" I cried, "Let this cup pass from me."

"I thought you longed to know Me," I heard my Savior sigh.

"Oh, I do, my Lord, but must I be betrayed? There must be another way."

"I will deliver you, if that is what you ask, but the only way to know me is to drink from my glass."

The struggle within me grew, for I wanted to know my King. So I humbled my fearful spirit, and said,

"Okay Lord, I will accept anything."

Betrayal began to rear its ugly head and in the midst, I heard a voice; this is what it said:

"As often as you drink, drink in remembrance of Me. For many trials are coming, but drink only in remembrance of Me."

As I drank from the cup of my Lord – I began a journey to know Him, like never I had before. His mercy flows like a river, and His love is yet untold.

So, I shall continue to drink, from a cup that's pure, beautiful and old. This cup cannot be seen with the eyes of this world, but drink of it I shall, as often as He wills.

To suffer with my Lord, is an honor I can't refuse; even if my life it cost, then my life I shall lose.

Towers Twin Fall

Towers twin filled, with many women and men, living their lives as in days gone by.

Sky-blue the day began, while terror flew above our great land. In a moment of time, America changed, as civilians died. Aboard American planes heroes were born and died in the same.

As the towers burned, the sky turned gray, hearts failed and the nation prayed. Our focus changed from our selfish thoughts, to seeking God with all of our hearts.

Tears falling, voices calling, "God help us, have mercy, have grace. God, come quickly and fill this place."

God bless America has filled our land. Flags flying, as man reaches out to man.

Love your neighbor, on which the law hangs, is becoming reality in the midst of our pain.

Policemen and firemen giving their lives. For greater love hath no man than to lay down his life for a friend.

The nation cries "Thank you." with tears in our eyes, as we remember your families, to know you have died. The day will come, when we stand before our God; and we will say thank you, as we worship our King.

America cries… "Let Freedom ring."

The Hero's Wives

To the wives of our heroes of this great land, I write a message with my pen in hand. My heart breaks, tears fill my eyes, my chest swells with pain, and my breath I can't find.

I think of my husband, the love of my life, as I think of our heroes and you, their wives. My mind is flooded with memories, the moments of my past. Memories of joy and happiness, tenderness and touches, sweet whispers, passionate kisses, moments of laughter, flow like a river. As I count my blessings and sadness, I count your losses, tears flowing. There is nothing that I can say that could even begin to ease your pain.

I can only tell you that I give my heart in moments of prayer, as I asked God, to let me help bear your burden. So, I lay before our great God and offered myself as a vessel, in memory of you and your family. Like a fountain, I pour out my soul. My heart aches and my body trembles, as I allow myself to suffer as a shadow of you.

My hope for you, is that you will always carry the memories of love, laughter and passion, in light of these great men, who shall forever live in hearts broken within. Amen.

Rain on
Me

The rain falls while the wind blows. A misty haze is seen all around. The creation speaks aloud what is unseen; from the heavens to the ground.

Like love falling, I can hear You calling. I see Your desire is to rain on me. Blow Spirit blow. Reign God reign. Arise bride arise.

Come forth old Word within me. Break free. Manifest. Bring forth the unseen. Come harvest of God's Word and forever feed me.

Gotta Run

How time can fly when there's work to be done; people, places, things gotta run.

I think of You often, longing to be with You, while time flies and work is done; people, places, things gotta run.

Just for a moment, I stopped for a quick, "I love and miss You", while time flies, and work is done; people, places, things gotta run.

I hear You calling. You softly speak my name. While time flies, and work is done; people, places, things gotta run.

Steal away, steal away! Don't let this moment pass. "I long for you," I hear Him say – "Stop!"

Togetherness…….at last.

No One Can Compare

Nothing – no, there is no one who can compare. No other love so true as You. You are truth. You are Love.

The way You know me is unimaginable. Your greatness is ever being revealed. My soul pants to know You more. With a word, You can take away my breath. Truly, I am melted like wax.

For even the deepest part of me, is seen by You. No one can compare. There is no other love so true as You.

My mind keeps wanting to hurry, towards destiny. But my heart knows destiny is like a dance in rhythm, and it shall play its perfect song, in perfect time and not a moment too soon. For the joy of the journey is found in the present, not in seeking the end.

Ever Blowing Wind

I can hear You everywhere, I seem to find You in every voice, every note, and every sound.

My eyes have begun to see You. I am amazed at how blind I have been. Yet now, even now, my sight is very dim.

More and more You reveal Yourself to me. More and more I long to know You. Your ways of language are without end. Your voice covers the earth, like an ever blowing wind.

Revive me. Change me. Mold me. Wake me up. For I want to know You more.

Remember Me in My Travail

Like a mother, remember me in my travail. Cause me to give birth in due time. Extend Your peace to me like a river. Cause me to carry Your sons and daughters, in my heart, until the day of the Lord.

Like a river, they shall break forth. Let me nurse them at the breast of love, acceptance and mercy. Let me give away the pure milk of Your love. Burn in my bones while love flows down. Let me bring them to You. Cause joy to flow, as a child who is dandled upon the knees. For on my knees I remember them all. Let my heart rejoice to see Your will fulfilled.

ANGELA Q. BERTONE

Shadows

For the prophets and the law, are a shadow of things to come. What is a shadow, and where is its coming?

It is an image, and an outline, of the Truth to come. It casts its form upon those to whom it is sent. A shadow is cast by light, yet in its nature is darkness.

Like the coolness, found in the shade of a grand oak tree, we all seek it for rest.

Unlike the shade of the oak tree, in this shadow no rest is found. For in the law, sin reigns, and the cost of it is death in the ground.

Arise, awake, oh sleeper. The Lord has come, and the Truth is here. Enter thou into His rest. You'll find rest in Him alone. Come out of the shadows. Find true rest in Him. Come forth manifestations. the Light has come. The shadows are seen no longer. Love, Truth, and Peace are here. The Word of God has risen, is manifested, and alive. Arise.

Thine Eyes

Give me Thine eyes, and cause me to see, others with Your love, the way You look at me. Cause my lips to speak, of Your love and Your beauty. Cause my eyes to see Your hand upon every man.

Open up my heart, and fill it with understanding. Deliver me from the knowledge of good and evil. Fill me up with Your mercy, over and ever flowing.

You alone are God, and judgment belongs to You. You alone are God, there is nothing man can do. Deliver us I pray, and restore us to Yourself. Give me eyes of love, and cause my lips to speak Your truth.

Oh Father, I thank You for opening up my heart, and causing the dam I built so long ago to break. Let this new life flow. The walls that I had built deep within my soul, have fallen hard, my wounded heart now seen. You used the one I love the most, to cause the wall to fall. Idolatry has lost its grip and You have set me free. From the lips where love does flow, came my painful blow.

In weakness, I felt my stomach turn, and blood began to flow. My memories of my past were sealed forgotten and left alone. I buried them long ago in a grave deep and wide: every time a word of rejection was spoken, it filtered it in my mind.

I thought I had rid myself of these ugly pains, when You lifted them from my heart. Yet it didn't take long and I discovered that they were also hidden in the recesses of my brain.

In deception I covered them all, hoping they would wane but from the God of resurrection they came to life again.

Somehow, I know that You had done this, to bring new life to me; but I must first face the lies or they will bury me. So I look at them, each of them, one by one, and face my fears. I now forsake the fear of man and trust in You alone.

"Ugly duckling, unbecoming, bonny and weak, different and shameful, who would want you? For you're a thin and lanky child, where did you come from?"

Words like a flood seem to drown me, in a river of rejection. When I heard the Father say,

"Look to Me for reflection. The world will tell you many things to kill your wounded soul, but I came to give you life and make you completely whole.

You have looked to others to feel acceptance and love, when only I can fill you up with what you are longing for. Hide and cover no longer to live, but yield yourself to Me. You shall find a hidden treasure beneath this ugly sea."

"Deep inside of every man is this longing to be loved, but there is only one true God who brings such hopeful yield."

"In every man is a measure, and I will make it grow like the flowers in My garden; it is for Me to know when to shine and when to rain and when to break-forth life. In due season, in the cycle, and yes even in the night, under the earth a hidden treasure breaks free into the light."

"I know this horrid pain you feel, for I walked upon the same earth. I did drink of your cup and on the cross cried 'I thirst'. I too was rejected and no beauty was found by them in Me; for My appearance was not lovely through the eyes of man. It was the eyes of My Father that never left My face. For it is His affection that is set on Me with grace."

"Because of His mercy and His grace, for a moment, He turned to look away; darkness fell upon the earth, tears streamed down Our face and in an instant, We set the captives free".

"My eyes are ever upon you, and your beauty I cannot resist. I came to live in your heart, for in you I delight. So, take your rest and lean on Me as I carry you through this night."

Walk Upon the Water

Teach me oh Lord, how in the sea of pain, to walk upon the water, and trust upon Your name.

When the sea is tossed, and the wind will not be still, to walk in perfect peace, and love others still.

For You will use mine enemies, and You will use my friends, to mold and to shape me from the beginning to the end.

Have mercy on me Lord, when my lover you must use, to transform the hardest part of me, and my heart begins to ooze.

In the deepest pains, and hardest trials of life, give me more grace to see You in the darkest of these nights.

For if my eyes are upon You, and your heart is what I see, I can drink the cup with You, for You drank it for me.

For You alone are worthy, and there is none other. Only You can save me from my judgments, and cause me to love my brother.

Two Sides

Thank you for seeing the little girl in me, for not holding me bound. You alone deliver me from all the wickedness found in me; that had purposed to hold me down.

Two sides are living, beating like the rhythm in my heart. You are gracious to see me and cover my naked parts. You cover me with grace and give me mercy too. You are my Father, and I find Love in You.

You searched the deepest part of me, and try me at your will; not so you can punish me, for you know that I will fail.

You show me my fallen nature, so I can see Your love. You seek to open my eyes, to show me Your view from above.

Blameless

Make me blameless and judgment free. Cause understanding to reign in me.

Cause my eyes to look with love, and see others from above.

Change my heart, deliver me, give me compassion and in me live.

My heart seeks justice and to be fair, ever hungry for right and wrong. Rescue me Lord I pray, cause me to seek mercy and more grace.

Change me, transform me, have mercy oh Lord. Make me a vessel for Love to flow, blameless, spotless and whole.

The Place Where Love Is Found

Your voice I long to hear; the memories I hold dear. The sound deep and strong, for that is what I long.

When I hear You call my name, it's all that I can do to stop my very breath, and focus upon You.

My heart beats strong; stronger still, at the wonderful sounds. They radiate from this place where only Love is found.

Oil Poured Forth

Oil poured forth to light a fire, to make bright the path. Oil poured forth, a healing to bring upon the wounds of the past.

Oil poured forth on dry and broken hands, to comfort the pains of the work wrought by man.

A softening, a pouring out, to break the toughest places. Hear our cry, make and prepare the way for His precious graces.

Fill me up. Poor me out. Use me Lord, I pray! Cause me to be used of my Master, every single day.

In the Heart of Man

In the heart of man, many things are found: love and laughter, joy and peace, echo the sounds.

Pain and sorrow is often seen beneath the happiness. Struggle seems to follow, to rush away the bliss.

To struggle is not the answer. For in the sorrow and the pain, counsel and wisdom are birthed, in such an awful rain.

Eternity was placed by God, in the heart of man. Stop to look and see this mystery of His plan.

Aleph and Tav, God alone is He. He spoke light and darkness, and gave them both to see.

Seek not only the joys of this life, but seek to know the Truth. In this you will find a mystery called pain, and know that it is only God in Whom all Truth reigns.

He Is My Strength

Knots rolling, pain forming, walls within stand tall. My spirit fights, my flesh seems to win, *fight harder*, still I try. Call forth His word inside.

"Arise!" I call. Acknowledging Him. Yielding myself to God within.

He is my strength, for I am weak.   Searching, searching, searching for peace.

You alone are God, You alone. Your love is great, and unimaginable. Break me Lord! I must pray, for I know there is no other way. So break me Lord and pour out Your grace, I surrender and cry.

"Mercy, mercy!" my soul cries. There is nothing else I can trust. Your mercies are great, my Lord, my God, rely on You I must.

Have mercy on me I pray. Let them be new each and every day. You search me Lord, and show me my ways. "Mercy, mercy!" my soul cries.

Every time my eyes see, all I can ask is mercy on me. Thank you God, for You truly are great! No other love compares. My soul cries to You, because You alone are the One who truly cares.

Cover Me

You hear my cry and comfort me. I drink in remembrance of You. You withdrew yourself from the one You love, and You could do no wrong.

The pain in Your heart Father, is inexpressible. The pain I suffer could bring me to self-destruction, but You had mercy on me.

You used my pain, and helped me to know You. Your love amazes me. Every mind of every man combined, cannot imagine Your great love and tender mercies.

You've covered me in Your grace, and You are teaching me Your ways. Strengthen me and strengthen my days.

Cause me to walk after You, and to walk in Your statutes. Show me how to honor Your Name. You alone are God. You alone are worthy of praise.

Your strength I cannot comprehend. Great and awesome is Your love.

I pray I can be faithful. Lord will you change my heart and the wickedness it holds?

For every time I am hurt or smitten, my thoughts are continually evil.

Thank You for Your mercy. Tie me to Your altar, and kill the nature in me. Cause me to bless and not curse. Birth in me pity not hate. Fill me with Your mercy and grace.

His Will Fulfilled

As I stood before my King to see what desire was in His heart for me, I looked around in this awesome place, and found everything where it should be, perfect and in its place. The gates of pearl, and streets of gold, the River of Life, and love untold.

Again I looked into His heart ablaze, with love and wondered: *What gift could I bring before my King?* I looked and saw in His heart an empty place, where the fire once burned bright. I turn my face in disbelief; what pain I saw, unspeakable grief.

He saw me look away and asked; *"Oh my bride you're here at last: What is your desire? What would you ask? For I am well pleased with you, My love. Ask whatever you will, and it is yours."*

"Oh my Lord and my King, if I could ask but just one thing. Bid me Lord, and I will ask, that my joy may be full at last."

With eyes of love, yet longing still, He bid me yet again. *"Your desire, my bride, I long to give to thee, for your beauty is far greater than any queen."*

I looked into His heart once more, and felt the pain and grief. And as I trembled in His presence, I opened my mouth to speak.

"That empty place that once burned bright, were pain and grief I see; could I go past the fire of love, and fill that place in Thee?"

"Oh, that place once burned bright; that is true. But you My love have filled My Heart with fire and passion blazing. Ask for something for you. Ask again anything you will, and I will give it to thee."

"Oh my King, if you permit, I will ask again. But if I ask whatever I will, will you give it to me?"

"Ask, my love, whatever, and I will give it to thee."

And so I opened my mouth to speak, trembling still I spoke. "I ask for the sons of men, all the souls, lost in sin. Can I give away this love that You have so freely given unto me?"

The fire in His heart burst into flames, with love like I had never seen. The fire burned so bright, His face I could not see. I fell at His feet to worship His Holiness. With tender mercies, He reached down and took me by my hand. Up, up, up, past the flames - and there - I saw His face again. With love unspeakable we looked into each other's eyes.

Tears flowed down His face. As I reached to wipe them away, I looked in His eyes once more, when in the reflection of His tears, I saw a river of people. All the sons of men, bowing down before Him.

Every knee bowed, every tongue confessed: "Jesus is Lord."

"Holy, Holy, Wholly is King Jesus!" I heard the angels cry.

Oh what joy unspeakable, full at last, on earth as it is in heaven. Amen!

Lost Child's Cry

I can take the darkness no longer. My hands have grown weary groping in this bottomless pit. Callouses snag my clothes and bloody hand-prints show clear my path. I long to caress Your face, but now, shame covers me and I fear You would no longer love me. My form has been twisted under the weight of the night. Dreams that were once filled with color and hope, have faded to black and white. These dark forms pull at me, seeking for my attention; I cover my eyes hoping they will give up and leave me be.

Who has stopped the earth from its spinning, and locked me in this cold dark winter? Will there be a remedy, or shall the sun ever be darkened? How long shall time continue to stand still? Must I accept that the sun has gone down on me, and forgotten that spring desires to live? Even the shadows are frozen in this space and time. No wait! Do they move? I wonder, is it me, that trembles in their presence?

Is there none who saves? Have all fallen? Must I take a risk and rise against this darkness, search for the Son and beacon Him to shine again?

Who has closed the door on hope, or has she even knocked? Maybe it is not dark-- maybe I am blind. Can anyone tell me, did the sun go down, or did my eyes grow dim?

"Hello!!! Is anyone there?"

Maybe they are, and my ears are none for the hearing, or maybe my voice is mute, even when I call.

"Hello!! Is anyone there? Am I alone? Hello!!"

If only I had a mother, she would help me. I know I had a mother once. I recall her touch. She was soft, and her scent was the scent of frankincense and myrrh. Her hair was like spun gold, and it moved like the wind. You should have seen her as she fed the sheep in the field, and then moved up the hills. Her feet seemed to dance, and the young goats followed her up to the mountains. The jewels that graced her neck, were her prayers for such as me. She placed lilies in her hair that gave striking contrast next to her dark skin. None could compare to her beauty, and no vanity could be found in her gaze.

She cared for her neighbor, the poor, and the stranger. Her voice was eternally sweeter than honey, yet she carried the boldness of the Lion with courage and nobility.

Her garments were fine linen, and her robes were royal. Swift were her feet to carry good news to all the nations.

When she held my hand, I could feel the beat of her heart, strong and true. She had dove's eyes, and on her brow she wore a crown. Her belt was Truth and her feet she washed in the waters of peace. The kisses of her lips were like the Rose of Sharon upon my fevered brow.

Once I was lost in the woods, and she found me. Her voice calling was like the warmth of the morning sun that chased away the frozen dew that blanketed my broken skin. None could ever compare to her. She has been called a mother to all, for she knew not a stranger.

"Every child is His and therefore I love them," she would say.

Her words were few, but they were warm and true. She fed upon wisdom and understanding, and no guile flowed from her fountain. Her husband was known in the gates, and His garments were kingly. He had marked her with His glory, and placed His ring upon her hand. ˙ *"Betrothed to His Beloved"* was sung across the land.

"What a wonderful world," she exclaimed, as she looked up to the clear blue sky.

Her teeth were like the white of the clouds, and her eyes found glory in the night. A rainbow she searched for in every storm: dancing in the rain for heaven's dew. She glistened as the rain sparkled like diamonds upon her face.

The trees of green and the rivers of blue all gave her joy; but the wonder that filled her eyes was always the love for His children. She was never in lack of compassion or inspiration; for she carried her Father's heart inside her, as a hidden treasure.

Oh, if my eyes could behold her again. When this night fell, and time stood still, she was lost. Though I called or cried, her voice I could not find. Comfort had abandoned mankind, and the rules of traditions swallowed the land. The rivers forgot to flow, and the wells ran dry. All day and night my soul does cry.

Where has she gone? If only I could rescue her like she rescued me. I heard whispers in the darkness that she had been poisoned by the trickery of reason and lost her way. Is it true? How can the truth be found in this darkness? This land is the land of the forgotten, I presume.

I think there was a time when she spoke of faith, hope and love. Love I recall, but faith and hope I am unable to recognize.

Is love enough when coupled with desire? She said my heart held the keys to all I would ever need to know.

I am shaken like a reed in the wind. Where do I turn and can my heart hear me? Maybe she spoke a truth, a secret hidden. She said there is a treasure in me, and even a kingdom.

How do I look within when my eyes are blind? If it responds, how can I perceive, with ears that are dull?

Oh if I had wings and could fly away, yet without sight I would only fall in the dust. I roll from left to right in this darkness yet, something in me calls. I began to kick and scream. I call her name, and kick again.

No longer can I take the night, and to my eyes I proclaim: "Oh eyes of mine, take your sight and summon your wings! Find this kingdom and take your reign."

Suddenly the earth beneath me trembled, and the walls broke, with cracks and creeks. Now I spin around yelling inside and out.

No longer shall I wait or grope in the dark. I shall arise and find a way.Reason has failed me, so I call on the King who lives in this kingdom inside me.

"Oh King of Kings, if you live, hear my cry for mercy. I am hurt and shy; but my mother gave me a flask of boldness. So, I drink it now, and cry in the dark. Rescue me I pray. Be my soul provider and heal my lands. Release me from these chains of hopelessness. I remember she spoke of your light, and said no darkness could rise against you. Are you there Oh King? I am calling."

The darkness spoke up and declared, "There is no such thing as light, for it has flown away. No hope lives here, for I am the void of all life."

I refused to listen to the darkness, so in my brokenness I called again. Suddenly my skin began to tremble and fall away.

Like a snake I was shedding my outer garment. I tried to hold on, but the dust of my form slipped through my fingers. Light pierced my eyes, and darkness fled. The shadows melted, and the clock stuck twelve.

The sound of a drum and trumpet began to play, and I heard an angel sing. "My child here I am."

This voice I recall. Memories flooded my soul. The door of my heart flung open wide, and the Lion stood tall in the way. Faith and hope flew with wings and dusted my form. I was made new. A songbird gave me a voice, and an eagle lifted my wings. The wind began to blow, and butterflies ushered her in. Her name was written on her head and it was Beloved. The mother of all, dressed in her garment of humility, and crowned with His love. She lifted me up, and presented me to the Lion.

His eyes were aflame, and looked right into my heart.

"You are home at last." He cried and held me tight. "This is the day of your salvation, and the day of My joy. For today the joy of Heaven is full and the earth rejoices even as the heavens. The promise and reconciliation are come, and The Father's will has been revealed; and to His Kingdom, there is no end."

Her Blood Cried, "Mercy"

Are you ready? Ready for the perfect storm? Not like any storm of the past. Oh yes, the flood waters shall roll, but not like the days of old. The covenant shall be seen but not in colors faded. The brightness of His love is royal and deep. Are you ready? This storm is from the underneath; waters of the deep, rising up at the setting of the Son. Where shall He lay His glorious head and unto whom shall He confide? Is there one who would trust Him to break and mold her and abide? Is there one of a broken and contrite soul? Is there a spirit to whom He can reveal His secrets untold?

Deep mysteries of old, hidden from the intellect, but freely given to the poor in spirit. Hungry and thirsty she shall be, and her thirst can be quenched by none other than Him. The storm inside of her weary soul, that bid her not to rest, was the storm that fell from the heart of God, at the one who found no rest. She alone has heard His cries, and she alone has pity. For she herself did long ago, drink of the same cups, called "Bitter and Heavy". In her sorrow and blindness, she called upon the King. Mercy she sought beyond her words, for her deaf ears had stolen her speech.

In darkness bound while dying alone, soaked in blood stained garments, her life did slip from her frame, when His eyes found pity on her. He had heard the blood upon the ground cry out through her silence, for her lips had found no sound.

He flew with wings and covered her frame, and proclaimed these words of compassion: "When ye die in your own blood, live ye, live, I say".

He breathed the breath of His lungs upon her, and wiped her tears away. He cleansed her with hyssop, washed her face, and sang a song of healing. Away He did take her from her grave, shallow and without honor; to a place of her hiding and sealed her behind the gates of safety.

As the days passed by, and her soul grew wise from abiding in His garden; she overheard His heart's song cry and from that day did tarry. His love had healed her, and filled her soul: now flowing and overflowing. She purposed out her heart that day to find for Him a solace. For in that day, her heart did hear the cries of His longing soul. She realized the pain He carried was for the wayward souls.

Though with Him she tarried, and her soul was filled with love, she found another hunger abiding in His soul. This was a hunger unlike any other; a hunger to find the lost. The lost she wept for day and night and sought the ancient scrolls; seeking for answers, maps or writings to deliver the ones He loved.

"The blood!" she cried, "I have found the ransom. The ransom of the Son. The Lamb of God who gave His life and paid the sinners toll."

For all who answered to His call, He cleansed and did restore. However, from the blind and deaf no answer echoed back. The children lost and seemed forgotten, their numbers were untold.

Then she remembered her story, of how He saved her soul. Blind and deaf, dying in blood, no voice to answer His call. He had mercy, and pitied her. Her deaf ears told her nothing of His coming, but still He saved her soul. Mercy! It was His mercy and love untold that saved my soul. His love laid down for me, healed me, cleansed and made me whole. He gave me His all and I shall not delay and give my life for Him. This mercy that He gave to me, I gladly shall lay down. I give it now to my Savior to bring before the courts, for the ones who cannot see or hear, and have no hope of His call.

For I too was blind and deaf, with no voice to answer at all. So take My mercy, and give it now so My Father's10 heart can be whole.

"Not one missing," I heard Him say was the will of my Father's soul.

So I believe like my Father Abraham, that nothing is impossible for Thee. Holy! Cry wholly! And let His will now be, on earth as it is in heaven and glory their eyes shall see. Let The Whole be reunited and not one missing for He alone is holy.

Postscript

Thank you for sharing in my journey of intimacy with our Lord and Savior Jesus Christ.   I have found that the pathway to intimacy is paved with the footsteps of sorrow and suffering.

I now know that suffering is a precious part of life that teaches me truths that cannot be found by any other means. The pain of sorrow is not worthy to be compared to the glory that is hidden within.

Let the broken places in your heart lead you into the Truth that has been locked beneath the fears. You too can find freedom in His perfect love and live fearless. Allow the King of the brokenhearted to give you beauty for your ashes and He shall shine His light of love through you for the world to see. For if we suffer with Him, shall we not also reign with Him.

About the Author

Born and raised in Louisiana with her five sisters, Angela cherishes the memories of her life growing up in the melting pot of that area's culture. From her mother, Sarah, came Angela's love of cooking and storytelling; her father, Louis, instilled in her a love of hunting and the outdoors. She can recall experiences with God that took place at the age of four, and she had a supernatural encounter with Jesus when she was fourteen. Over the years, she has forged a unique biblical perspective by digging deep into the significance of words, numbers, creation, and the human body. In 1985, Angela married her best friend and hunting buddy, Michael Sr. Beside their two adult children, they also presently have four grandchildren. Michael and Angela are ordained ministers who have traveled together across America, teaching and demonstrating revolutionary truths about the human body and how it relates to our spirituality. Moreover, as an author and spiritual life coach, Angela travels nationally and internationally, bringing her revolutionary work to the world. It is her desire to change the way individuals view emotions, allowing their hearts to heal as they learn to process emotions in a healthy manner.

Angela facilitates over 400 personal sessions per year, with miracles following. Breaking unhealthy life cycles that have been trapped in the subconscious has yielded miraculous healing to numerous recipients. She has seen cancers die, tumors disappear, a dead bladder come to life, PTSD disappear, marriages heal, and symptoms of fibromyalgia and food allergies cease. Her life coaching has set people free from codependent and selfdestructive relationship patterns.

You can follow her on Facebook, Twitter, PodOmatic, Patreon and iTunes.

Angela's website is **www.angelabertone.com**

www.ingramcontent.com/pod-product-compliance
Lightning Source LLC
Chambersburg PA
CBHW031524040426
42445CB00009B/382